Original title:
The Pear's Promise

Copyright © 2025 Creative Arts Management OÜ
All rights reserved.

Author: Eleanor Prescott
ISBN HARDBACK: 978-1-80586-249-9
ISBN PAPERBACK: 978-1-80586-721-0

The Secret Life of Orchard Dreams

In a tree where giggles grow,
Fruits conspire on the low.
Pears in coats of green disguise,
Joke about the sunny skies.

Squirrels tease with acorn glee,
Sipping dew as if it's tea.
Listen close, the whispers spread,
"Why did the fruit go to bed?"

"Oh, it couldn't take the heat,
Its friends were far too sweet!"
Laughter hangs upon the breeze,
While bees buzz with such great ease.

As autumn casts a golden spell,
The orchard's tales blend oh-so-well.
With laughter ripe and jokes to share,
It's the happiest fruit affair!

Green Confessions of the Heart

In a patch of emerald sheen,
A fruit spilled secrets, so serene.
"I love a tree with branches wide,
But I'd rather roll than hide!"

"Why chase the wind," the apple said,
"Just sit with me and rest your head."
Pears giggled, hanging all around,
Spreading joy without a sound.

"Don't tell the roots, but grapes get shy,
When the sun decides to say goodbye."
Leaves rustle, sharing silly dreams,
While everyone bursts at the seams.

They plan a dance under the stars,
With fruit in slippers, no need for cars!
It's a circus of colors, bold and bright,
Where laughter echoes through the night!

Sunlit Pathways of Potential

On sunlit paths, where laughter twirls,
A fruit with secrets gives sly little swirls.
Each step we take, with giggles and glee,
Leads us to wonders as bright as can be.

Among the trees, mischievous sprites,
Whisper sweet tales of charming delights.
With every bend, there's a tasty surprise,
A treasure awaits in the clear blue skies.

Fragrant Oaths in Nature

In gardens lush, the scents unite,
Breezes carry whispers, oh what a sight!
Promises bloom, with petals so fine,
Fragrant oaths drawn, in sun's warm shine.

The bees conspire, with giggles galore,
Pollen parties behind every door.
Nature's a joker, full of silly schemes,
Where blossoms giggle and dance in dreams.

Hopes Woven in Petals

With threads of hope, petals softly weave,
Stories of joy, oh how they deceive!
A playful breeze teases each flower,
While crickets chant, in their nightly hour.

Hopes spun like candy, sweet on the tongue,
While flowers in slippers do a jig, so young.
They wink and they nod, in bright colors clad,
Creating a spectacle, oh it's so rad!

The Dance of Juicy Dreams

In the orchard's embrace, where sweetness abounds,
Fruitful dreams sway, with jubilant sounds.
Each juicy giggle bursts forth with glee,
As the world spins around, so funny and free.

Beneath the great sky, clouds share a laugh,
As the fruits wobble like a carefree calf.
In a whimsical waltz, they twirl and they play,
Celebrating the joys of a sun-kissed day.

A Tale of Hidden Growth

In the garden where shadows dwell,
A secret fruit began to swell.
With whispers soft, it took a chance,
To jig and jive, and do a dance.

The squirrels giggled at its style,
Winking paws and cheeky smile.
But roots deep down, they knew the game,
One day they'd shout its juicy name.

Charting the Course of Fruition

A map was drawn by tiny hands,
To find the treasure in fertile lands.
X marked the spot, a tree quite bold,
With dreams of sweetness, green and gold.

The leaves conspired, shushed and shy,
"Adventure awaits," they swayed nearby.
But each new sprout must bide its time,
Or risk fate's jest, a twist or climb.

Whispering Leaves and Wishes

The leaves all gathered for a chat,
To gossip 'bout the new-born brat.
"Just wait," they rustled, "he'll soon appear,
With laughter ripe and fruity cheer."

They dreamed of pies and jolly jams,
Of summer days and picnic clams.
Yet in the breeze, through giggles loud,
They all embraced their leafy crowd.

Embracing Sun-kissed Horizons

Beneath the sun, they painted dreams,
Of shiny skins and sugary creams.
With laughter bursting, seeds took flight,
A fruity future shining bright.

So as they played, in evening's glow,
The world spun fast, with joy on show.
For soon enough, the time would come,
To prove that being silly's fun.

Beneath the Boughs of Hope

In a tree where fruits conspire,
A pear joked, 'I'm an acquired taste!'
Laughter echoed, roots in the mire,
Swaying whimsically, none in haste.

A squirrel snickered, plucked his snack,
'This place is ripe, but where's my lunch?'
The pear replied with cheeky clack,
'Bring your own nuts, I'm not your crunch!'

Secrets of the Orchard

In the orchard where secrets hide,
A pear spilled tales of yesterday's fun.
'Why did the apple run and slide?
To catch a breeze - oh what a pun!'

With giggles bubbling like spring dew,
The fruits shared stories, quite absurd.
A grape chimed in, 'I once flew too!'
All laughed aloud, their joy unstirred.

The Ripening Truth

A pear with dreams so bold and bright,
Declared, 'I'll be the star of the feast!'
The others chuckled, 'What a sight!'
'You best be ready to be a beast!'

So ripe it twirled, full of delight,
Yet fell with a splat, oh what a scene!
'No crown for you,' the orchard took flight,
A pear that giggled, still evergreen.

Lush Legacy Adrift

A pear that thought it ruled the grove,
Declared, 'I'm fancy, none can compare!'
But snickered leaves played peek-a-boo,
And teased it so, 'Just don't show flair!'

As fruits swayed in comical play,
A kiwi hollered, 'Now that's in style!'
The pear, still grand, just had to stay,
With laughter bursting, mile after mile.

Delicate Futures in Every Drop

Beneath the tree, hopes pop like fizz,
Juicy dreams dangle, oh what a whizz!
Each drip of dew, a plan so sly,
Giggles grow sweet as fruit cries, 'Try!'

Dances of bees, a buzz so grand,
Whispering secrets, making their stand.
The branches sway, a twist of fate,
Puns and laughs, we can hardly wait!

The Orchard's Silent Oath

In a quiet grove, whispers take flight,
Trees share jokes in soft moonlight.
A vow so silly, in bark and root,
Promising pears a life so cute.

Leaves chuckle softly, rustling the air,
As they plot schemes to catch us unaware.
Who knew fruit could be such a prank?
Nature's jesters, to all, they'd prank!

Entwined in Nature's Embrace

Twisting vines, they giggle and twirl,
A wobbly dance, oh how they swirl!
With each small bud, a secret is spun,
Nature's own jest, oh what fun!

Laughter erupts as blooms burst wide,
Petals like confetti, happy and tied.
Each fruit a punchline, ripe with delight,
Oh, join in the revel, from morning till night!

Fruits of Faith and Patience

With every season, we wait and grin,
For nature's joke to just begin.
A tickle of sun, a splash of rain,
Hazards of humor in every grain.

Tending our hopes with shovels and spite,
Laughter sprouts up, oh what a sight!
The harvest of giggles, juicy and bright,
Baskets of joy, all set for a bite!

A Harvest Yet to Come

In the garden, dreams take root,
A fruit with a silly pursuit.
It giggles and wiggles, oh so bright,
Waiting for fate to bring delight.

Jokes in the sunlight, laughter on leaves,
It tickles the vines, as nature believes.
Promises hanging, light as a jest,
With every new breeze, they dance with zest.

The Weight of Anticipation

A heavy heart in a light green shell,
Wonders of sweetness, oh can you tell?
Each day it waits, growing dreams within,
Like a balloon that's begging to spin.

Tickling the branches, it plays hide and seek,
Amidst the chirping, it starts to freak.
"Oh, me? I'm ripe! Just look at my skin!"
But everyone knows it's a fruit of a grin.

Echoes of Sweetness

Echoes of laughter bounce through the leaves,
Every whisper of wind, a joke that deceives.
"Am I sweet?" asks the fruit with a pout,
"Just take a bite! What's it all about?"

Each moment it spends, teasing the sun,
Knowing soon enough, life will be fun.
From branch to branch, it swings with glee,
A fruity comedian, wild and free.

Dreams Ripening in the Breeze

In the gentle sway of a balmy air,
Dreams are ripening, full of flair.
They blush in the sunshine, giggling away,
"Tomorrow, my friend, we'll have our day!"

Puns on the vine, with giggles galore,
As the fruit rolls laughter, it wants to explore.
With every gust that tickles a limb,
It grins and it chuckles, what a whim!

The Language of Unripened Dreams

In the orchard, whispering trees,
Dreams hang low with laughter and tease.
Wobbling fruits like clumsy clowns,
Pelt the ground with gentle frowns.

Each green orb a secret shared,
Jokes on branches, none prepared.
Tickled leaves giggle in delight,
As shadows dance in fading light.

Blossoms Beneath Shimmering Stars

Under stars that wink and sway,
Blossoms blush at dusk's ballet.
Petal pranks in moonlit creeks,
Nature's humor boldly speaks.

Buds like giggly children play,
Waiting for their big debut day.
All dressed up in colors bright,
Adventure waits to take its flight.

Fragrance of Hopes Yet to Bloom

Scents so sweet, yet still a tease,
Dreaming blooms in summer's breeze.
Tongues of nectar, laughter flows,
While bees debate when beauty shows.

Each day waits, a sly little grin,
Promising smiles to wear and spin.
Uncertain futures, a jesters' game,
In the garden of hopes aflame.

A Quiet Trust in Nature's Hand

Seeds lay down with secret wishes,
Quietly plotting devious swishes.
In silent trust, they hatch their plans,
Bouncing thoughts like playful fans.

Roots stretched deep, a ticklish riddle,
Nature's laugh is soft and brittle.
Underneath a green disguise,
Lies a world of bright surprise.

Guardians of the Crop

In the orchard, giggles reign,
Fruit spies in clouds, don't complain.
With every bump and silly fall,
They guard the crew, standing tall.

Squirrels plot their heist at dusk,
Sneaky faeries, what a fuss!
Juicy secrets in leafy hides,
Laughter bubbles while joy resides.

Each branch teases with ripened rest,
Who can munch on this? The best!
Old tales spun by wise old trees,
With tickling winds and buzzing bees.

Lemonade dreams dance on the breeze,
As giggling friends plan fruit-filled feasts.
In this place full of mirth,
Nature's treasure, unmeasured worth.

Sweet Anticipation in Quiet Moments

Beneath the stars, we gather 'round,
As moonlit fortune's here, we've found.
Expectations rise like morning dew,
Chasing shadows, what fun to pursue!

Whispers travel from leaf to leaf,
Every laugh hides a tiny belief.
With each tick of time, we await,
A surprise that's sure to be great!

Not a care for the time's slow crawl,
We share our secrets, one and all.
Rustling stories fill the night,
Dreams wrap us in pure delight.

As morning arrives, sweet treats in sight,
We feast on laughter, pure delight.
The sunbeams dance, and off we run,
To seek the treasures, oh what fun!

Whispers of Sweet Blossoms

In the breezy grove of laughter loud,
Petals plot their cheerful crowd.
With every blossom, secrets spun,
Nature's jokes, oh, what fun!

Bumblebees buzz with silly grace,
Chasing shadows in a flower race.
Each bright bud whispers its cheer,
Silly stories fill the air near.

The nightingale croons silly tunes,
While raccoons steal the silver spoons.
In this garden, where dreams are sown,
Joy's sweet blossom has brightly grown.

Humming with giggles and playful bops,
The fruits of joy are never stops.
Take a bite, and laughter will reign,
In every juicy, funny gain.

Fruitful Dreams Await

Under a fluffy cloud of glee,
Happy fruit dreams dance with me.
Moonlight plays upon bright skins,
Whimsical visions turn into spins.

With each tickle of a branch so bold,
A cheeky secret begins to unfold.
Fuzzy kids sneaking for supplies,
Bouncing off the trees, what a surprise!

Songs of harvest fill the air,
Chasing squirrels, we have our share.
From shy blossoms to ripe delight,
Fruitful giggles burst into flight.

So raise a cheer for fruits to grow,
For every bite, a giggling show.
With every season, we'll embrace,
The joyful harvest of silly grace!

Hushed Whispers Among the Leaves

In a garden full of chatter,
Leaves gossip with a swish.
A fruit with dreams of grandeur,
Might just fulfill a wish.

Beneath the branches swaying,
A secret giggle flows.
A pear is plotting mischief,
As the gentle breeze blows.

With raindrops as their dance floor,
And sunshine as their stage,
Each fruit has a plan ready,
To break free from this cage.

Watch out for those ripe whispers,
In the summer's sweltering heat.
For once they're off the branch,
They'll be ready for a treat!

Journey of a Coming Season

A tree stands tall and sturdy,
With branches stretched out wide.
Each bud is a little jester,
In nature's merry ride.

Spring brings a funny racket,
As blooms begin to prank.
With colors bright and cheerful,
They paint the world in dank.

The fruit just laughs and giggles,
As they swell with summer sun.
They know their time is coming,
For ripeness can be fun!

As seasons change and dance,
With routines oh so absurd,
This merry bunch is waiting,
Until their names are heard!

The Sun's Embrace on Young Fruit

A warm hug from the sunlight,
Makes young fruit grin and glow.
Each curve is filled with laughter,
As warmth begins to grow.

The sun plays peek-a-boo games,
With clouds up in the sky.
And all the little fruits chuckle,
As they reach up oh so high.

They dream of sunny picnics,
And pies fresh from the oven.
With every ray they're tickled,
By visions of sweet lovin'.

Such joy in every moments,
As laughter lights the air.
These cheeky little treasures,
Are a reason to declare!

Secrets Held in Velvet Skin

Beneath a coat of velvet,
A secret softly sighs.
Each fruit is a little joker,
Behind its rounded guise.

The skin may seem so proper,
But underneath, there's flair.
When cut, a burst of laughter,
With hints of sweet despair.

Neighbors try to guess the flavors,
With each and every bite.
But this playful little fruit,
Keeps its mysteries tight.

So gather round, dear friends,
With each slice and each share.
For laughter's in the secrets,
Hidden in the pear!

Tapestry of Green Inspirations

In a garden where giggles ignite,
Laughter sprouts in the warm sunlight.
The leaves wear hats, the roots do cheer,
A jolly plant party, bring on the beer!

Green beans dance in a conga line,
They wiggle and jiggle, oh so fine!
The carrots in capes, the radishes in gowns,
All joined in fun, without any frowns.

A tomato swung from a vine on high,
Shouting, 'Catch me if you can!' with a sly!
But slipped on a leaf, with a tomatoy squish,
Now that's a gardening dream gone swish!

With bees on trumpets, they buzz a tune,
Even the sunflowers started to croon.
In this tapestry, laughter is sown,
For in every plant, a joyfully grown.

The Sweetness of Anticipation

A tiny seed dreamed of the sky,
Wearing shades, oh my, oh my!
It plotted and schemed, with roots all curled,
To become the star of the vegetable world!

"Just wait!" it said, with a wink and a grin,
"I'll be the sweetest, let the fun begin!"
With sunlight smiling and rain drops, too,
It prepared for the best debut.

Neighbors laughed as it sprouted high,
"Look at that chap, it's reaching the sky!"
But little did they know, full of glee,
It would turn into fruit, oh wait and see!

Finally ripe, with a jolly bounce,
It shouted, "I'm here! Come take me, pounce!"
With cheeks all rosy and a flavor so bright,
It was fruity fun, oh what a sight!

From Blossom to Bounty

A flower bloomed, what a sight to see,
It shouted, "Look at me, so fancy and free!"
Dressed in petals, all colors astound,
It boogied on branches, spinning round and round!

Said the bud to the bee, "Come join my show,
We'll groove our way, we'll steal the whole show!"
They danced with the breeze, and hummed a tune,
The garden erupted, a floral cartoon!

Each bloom had dreams of juicy delight,
They giggled in whispers, "We'll be a sweet bite!"
With butterflies chuckling, life was so grand,
Nature's own laughter spread over the land!

When harvest came, oh what a sight,
A bounty of giggles, so soft and light!
From twirls to a feast, oh what a thrill,
With fruit on the table, laughter to spill!

Journey of a Little Seed

A small little seed had a wanderlust,
It dreamed of mountains and places to thrust.
With a wiggle and a giggle, it set on its way,
"Adventure awaits!" it would proudly say!

Rolling down hills, in a bumpy ol' cart,
It made friends with worms, played a funny part.
The earth was its home, with stories to tell,
Of roots and of sprouts, and the fun they'd dwell.

"Let's play hide and seek!" said a sprightly new sprout,
They peeked through the leaves, giggling about.
But the sunlight was strong, and the rain fell in streams,
In this garden of dreams, everyone beams!

So up it shot, with a bounce and a glee,
No longer a seed, oh, come look at me!
A twist and a shout, with branches held wide,
It bloomed with a chuckle, full of green pride!

Signatures in the Soil

In dainty rows, the seeds do slide,
With giggles from the earth, they hide.
Wiggly worms in a dance so slick,
Plan to take a new trick for a pick.

A jazz band plays beneath the grass,
Roots do a shimmy, they sure do sass.
Oh, how the critters do realign,
To throw a celebration, in sunshine shine.

The snails wear capes, the ants in hats,
All waiting for growth while munching on snacks.
With twinkling eyes, the veggies cheer,
In this soil party, there's nothing to fear!

As petals whirl like a disco ball,
Beneath this canopy, we'll all have a ball.
With each new sprout, a laugh unfolds,
In the garden of giggles, where fun never grows old!

The Weight of Sweet Anticipation

Oh, wait till they swell, the fruits divine,
Each day spent watching feels like a climb.
With hands on hips, we stare at the vines,
Musing about flavors, oh so fine!

The sun comes out with a cheerful grin,
While birds dive down, preparing to sing.
Every bud whispers secrets untold,
About the sweet bounty soon to behold.

We giggle at bees, so busy and round,
In this garden's realm, fun unbound.
The weight of the wait, it's such a thrill,
Like waiting for candy, or a jolly chill!

Frogs croak jokes in the warm summer heat,
All here to celebrate a harvest so sweet.
So let's dance with joy, for the time is near,
To taste all these wonders and toast with cheer!

Colors of Unseen Blessings

In the garden, hues do play,
Each blossom hides a funny cliché.
Daisies tickle the turf with glee,
While clouds drift by, looking like tea!

Lettuce rustles, and carrots grin,
With radish jokes, where to begin?
Oh, the kale can't hold its leafy laugh,
A salad to be, the giggles on half!

Twinkling petals in colors so bold,
Twist and twirl, as stories unfold.
The hidden joys, like whispers of fate,
Creep through the garden, never too late!

With butterflies dancing on fragile wings,
Each color sings of joy that it brings.
In this patch of wonders, all shades unite,
Creating a mosaic of sheer delight!

Fond Murmurs of the Grove

In the shady nook where laughter spills,
Trees share secrets and the breeze fulfills.
Squirrels chatter in a quirky debate,
Planning their hoard while munching on fate.

The boughs bend low, their whispers in rhyme,
Tickling each other with tales of old thyme.
How wild the stories these branches hold,
Adventures of nuts, both young and bold!

Each rustle of leaves is a cheeky jest,
As critters plot to put humor to test.
In this grove of smiles, worries can fade,
Where the punchlines grow in the cool shade!

With every soft swoosh, we join the fun,
Counting the giggles as warm as the sun.
Let's gather the whispers, let's make a toast,
To this joyful grove, where laughter's the most!

Nectar of Tomorrow's Bloom

A tree stands tall, with fruit so round,
It giggles softly, without a sound.
The wind whispers secrets, fun and free,
Of sweet surprises waiting for thee.

Sunshine dances on leaves, oh so bright,
While squirrels prepare for a nutty night.
Buds tremble with laughter, shaking with glee,
As they dream of the nectar, just wait and see!

Each blossom unfolds with a cheeky grin,
Promising sweetness, let the feast begin!
But nature just chuckles, keeping it sly,
"First, let's play hide-and-seek, oh my!"

When harvest dawns, the giggles resound,
As fruits tumble down, all joy unbound.
A basket of smiles, who knew it could be,
That joy grows in gardens, just wait and see!

A Promise in Every Seed

In the soil, a secret, a tale so grand,
Each little seed dreams of a future planned.
With a wink and a wiggle, it burrows deep,
Guarding its giggles, while we all sleep.

Rain drops like confetti, a party in air,
Each sprout is a dancer, with roots to share.
They twirl out of darkness, to the warm light,
Claiming the stage, what a joyful sight!

The sun gives a wink, golden and bright,
"Let's grow silly fruits, oh what a delight!"
The promise of laughter bubbles in bloom,
With fruits full of joy, their giggles consume.

Then one fateful day, the harvest draws near,
With laughter and snacks, oh the autumn cheer!
For what's life without taste, the thrill of a seed?
Let's celebrate giggles, come join in the feed!

Harvesting the Future

In a fuzzy patch, where goodies abound,
Fruitful delights are waiting to be found.
With baskets of joy, let's gather and play,
As laughter erupts in the bright sunny bay.

The apples are pouting, not ready to share,
While berries are blushing, hiding in flair.
"Don't rush!" shouts the grape, dangling so fine,
"Let's savor the moment, we'll be just divine!"

A squirrel comes hopping, with tales to unfold,
Bringing wild stories of treasures untold.
"Promise me sweets, I'll keep my jokes bright,
Join in my frolic, from morning to night!"

Harvesting laughter, our giggles take flight,
With each tiny fruit, we share pure delight.
A banquet of joy, let's savor the cheer,
With every sweet moment, the future is clear!

Beneath the Green Canopy

Under a green umbrella, shadows play,
A circus of critters are out for the day.
With squirrels in tutus, and bunnies that leap,
The fruits hide their secrets, tucked snug in sleep.

A jester of leaves wiggles with fun,
While berries look on, basking in sun.
Whispers of promises float on the breeze,
"Just wait for tomorrow, we'll tickle the trees!"

Giggling branches sway, as the breeze joins the game,
Each piece of fruit craves a slice of fame.
"Look at us gleaming, dressed up in hue,
A colorful banquet, for me and for you!"

So we gather together, beneath the grand dome,
To relish the magic, where laughter is home.
With each bite of delight, we'll savor the cheer,
For joy in the garden belongs to us here!

Nature's Pact of Abundance

In orchards bright, they giggle and sway,
Fruit insists on a comical play.
Round and jolly, they hide from despair,
While squirrels hold court, without a care.

With sun-kissed skins, they prank on the breeze,
Dropping hints of sweet, oh what a tease!
The bees bust those moves, they dance on the floor,
Laughing at life, they always want more.

Each green whisper and flirty breeze,
Tells of joy that's sure to please.
A merry band that simply won't quit,
In this lively patch, they never sit!

So raise a toast to their goofy schemes,
Nature's delight in our wildest dreams.
From garden's edge to the tree tops high,
In the world of fruit, you'll find the sky!

Shadows of Vital Promise

Beneath the branches, shadows play,
Tickling toes in a sunny ballet.
Where laughter echoes and giggles bloom,
Even the rocks wiggle, make room!

Frisky whispers drift through the leaves,
As nature crafts the best of thieves.
Robbers of sunlight, those cheeky little fruit,
Stealing hearts in their playful pursuit.

The sun grins wide, the moon rolls its eyes,
As fruit dare to flirt with the starry skies.
"Are we ripe enough yet?" they chuckle and tease,
While ants march on by, with crumbs and keys!

So let's join the fun, be silly and spry,
With shadows that dance and birds that fly.
In this playful garden where laughter is found,
Life's joyous moments always abound!

In Gardens of Tomorrow's Hope

In the garden of hope, the seeds drop and spin,
Ripe dreams whisper softly, "Come on in!"
Laughter erupts as the plants take a jig,
Bouncing and bobbing, so lively and big!

'Til carrots start tapping, and beans sing a tune,
Every sprout joins in, from sun up to moon.
Pumpkins roll over, just waiting to tease,
Beneath a grand sky filled with swaying trees.

Hope grows wild in this magical place,
As bees crack jokes, their pollen embraced.
From flowers to fruit, a comic delight,
Where every new day feels perfectly bright!

So dance with the daisies, and twirl with the thyme,
Find joy in each leaf, oh such wonderful rhyme!
For laughter is seed, you plant in a row,
In gardens of dreams, it's always a show!

Essence of Ripening Joy

In fields of joy where fruits do prance,
Each smiling peach leads a jolly dance.
They toss silly quips to the clouds up high,
Making mischief beneath the bright sky.

"Hey, we're sweet! Come take a bite!"
Merrily glowing in the warm sunlight.
Every day ripens, a giggle so grand,
As laughter bursts forth like grains of sand.

With every breeze that tickles the trees,
Nature's punchline brings us to our knees.
A vine walks into a bar, oh what a sight,
Telling jokes that bring fruit flies delight!

So let's toast our glasses with cherry-red cheer,
And celebrate life, with those we hold dear.
In a world of laughter, let worries be few,
For the essence of joy is just ripe for you!

Seeds of Promise in Spring's Embrace

In spring, we plant with subtle grace,
Hoping for fruit, a fruitful race.
But ants join in, a quirky parade,
Eating our dreams, oh how they invade!

Sunshine beams with a cheeky grin,
Encouraging seeds to dance and spin.
Yet little sprouts look up in doubt,
'We're just green snacks, what's this about?'

The gardener hums a cheerful tune,
While sparrows swoop as if in a swoon.
Each tiny sprout, a jester bright,
Yelling, 'Plant your hopes, it's going to be alright!'

So weeds come in, with fashion flair,
A wild, green party beyond compare.
With laughter echoing across the patch,
Let's hope soon fruit will hatch!

A Symphony of Green Goodness

In the garden, a concert grows,
With veggies jamming, as everyone knows.
Carrots groove, while peas in pods,
Swing to the rhythm, defecting the odds!

Tomatoes sway, all red and proud,
While lettuce cheers from the leafy crowd.
'Don't forget us!' cries a spry zucchini,
Dancing like a champ, all shiny and weeny!

The radishes waltz in their spicy clothes,
While chives play tunes with their leafy prods.
It's a veggie bash, with laughs galore,
Who knew that greens could have such rapport?

Yet beware the hungry critters' plot,
Mice dreaming of salad, oh, what a lot!
But joy prevails, it's a funny sight,
A garden fiesta that lasts through the night!

Beneath a Starlit Canopy

Under the stars, the garden sleeps,
But dreams of veggies sneak through the peeps.
Cucumbers whisper in the moonlight glow,
'Wouldn't it be fun to watch and grow?'

A radish twirls in its earthy bed,
'Plotting world takeovers, let us be fed!'
While moonbeams tickle the leaves so bright,
'We'll grow a salad to dazzle tonight!'

The cucumber grins, 'How about a dance?
With a vinaigrette splash, we'll take a chance!'
But then a bolt from the sky comes near,
And all the veggies shuffle in fear!

The stars just giggle, their bright eyes glint,
As veggies sway, 'We won't leave a hint!'
So laugh with the greens, in this cosmic scheme,
Beneath the starlit shine, they thrive in a dream!

Timeless Oaths of the Growing Season

With spring's first light, a pact is made,
Seeds and soil agree to invade.
'No pests allowed, we won't play nice,'
'Unless you bring compost, oh, that's our price!'

As sprouts emerge, they raise a toast,
'Here's to the beans that we love the most!
And sigh for the garlic, so bold and suave,
Let's grow together, it's the garden rave!'

But then the rains drop, a surprise shower,
Full of laughter, they thrive by the hour.
'We're not mere snacks; we're treasures, you see,
With flavor so grand, we're all meant to be!'

As summer rolls up, they dance like fools,
Signing oaths under sun-drenched jewels.
So join this jolly, growing affair,
With promises of harvest, oh what a rare flare!

Tending to the Promise Within

In the garden, a fruit took a stance,
Wobbling slightly, it danced its romance.
With a nod to the bees and a wink to the sun,
It dreamed of the harvest, oh what funny fun!

Belly full of laughter and cheeks full of glee,
It tickled the tadpoles with jokes near the tree.
Sprouting bright blossoms, it chuckled with glee,
'This isn't just fruit, it's pure comedy!'

Blushing in green, with a grin so wide,
It played hide-and-seek with the sun, ran with pride.
On a branch, it spun tales of what it would be,
A pie, a jam, or a fruity 'Whoopee!'

Through laughter-filled breezes, the promise grew sweet,
In a world filled with wonders, it skipped to its beat.
Each giggle a raindrop, each snicker a breeze,
It knew in its heart, it would bloom with great ease.

Feasts of the Mind's Eye

Sipping dew drops, a fruit munches cheer,
Dreaming of feasts that would soon draw near.
With a slapstick twist and a plump little jig,
It planned a grand banquet, oh what a big gig!

Imagining pies on a fanciful plate,
While squirrels chuckled at plans far too great.
'Caramel drizzles and whipped cream galore!'
It juggled the flavors, just begging for more.

With fizzing delight, it tossed fruit in air,
A wobbly dance with utmost flair.
'Banana's a joker, and grapes throw a party!'
It twirled 'round the orchard—'This meal won't be tardy!'

As shadows stretched long and the moon peeked through,

The fruit burst with laughter, its joy was so true.
In a banquet of whimsy, it feasted with pride,
For humor blooms sweeter when love's by its side.

Under the Canopy of Belief

In the shade of belief, where silliness sways,
The fruit pranced around in the sun's playful rays.
With leaves as its audience, it tickled the air,
'The world's a big joke—so let's share a pair!'

Bouncing like laughter on soft, grassy beds,
Tales spun like vines, from roots to their heads.
A chorus of giggles echoed up high,
As the fruit winked at clouds drifting by.

'Under this canopy, we'll conjure delight,
With shadows that dance in the warm summer night.
Let's stitch up the moonbeams, and weave stars with cheer,
A tapestry bright where magic draws near!'

And as twilight settled, the fruit said with glee,
'Life's one big joke, come chuckle with me!
We'll savor the moments, let silliness bloom,
In this glorious garden, there's always more room!'

Promises Woven Through Seasons

As spring whispered secrets, a promise took flight,
A fruit pondered life with a giggle so bright.
'We're weaving our futures, with laughter and zest,
Each season a chapter, let's put it to test!'

Summer sun blazed, and the fruit flew so high,
Did it tumble? It tripped! But oh, what a fly!
Cracking up daisies that rolled in the breeze,
'Falling's a laugh—if you land with such ease!'

When autumn shook hands with its russet tones,
The fruit played in piles of crunches and moans.
'Oh, the leaves are like jokes, falling bright in a swirl,
Each one a good punchline, in this colorful whirl!'

Then winter rolled in with a giggle and spin,
The fruit huddled close, with a wink and a grin.
'Each promise, each season, a story so sly,
Life's a big banquet; let's eat, drink, and fly!'

The Golden Glow of Tomorrow

In the tree so lush and green,
A fruit with a glimmering sheen.
It giggles as it hangs so high,
Saying, "I'm the apple of your eye!"

Every day it soaks the sun,
Winking with a playful pun.
"I'll be your snack, just wait and see,
A luscious feast, you'll want to squeeze!"

Old branches creak with a wise old tale,
Of fruity pranks and a silly male.
"Don't bite too soon, just take a glance,
I promise that I'll lead this dance!"

So when you stroll beneath the shade,
Know well the tricks that we have played.
A golden glow that's not quite ripe,
Will turn your snack into a type!

A Promise Written in Sap

In the grove, where laughter flows,
Sap drips down like secret prose.
"Write your hopes," the young tree said,
"On a leaf, don't be misled!"

A squirrel quipped, with nut in hand,
"Promises taste better than bland!"
As bees buzzed with cheerful glee,
They hummed, "Join our jamboree!"

The blossoms winked with fragrant tease,
"Bet we'll dangle in the breeze!
Just like dreams that float and sway,
We'll be sweet by the end of day!"

So gather 'round beneath this sky,
And hear the jest from branches high.
For laughter blooms like springtime's glow,
A sap-soaked promise we all know!

Secret Lives of the Orchard

In the orchard, whispers creep,
Where fruits plot and vines leap.
"What's the scoop with Mr. Pear?"
"Shh, don't tell, but he's quite rare!"

With the apples all in line,
"Mister Pear thinks he's divine!
Claims he's the king of all he sees,
But we know he's just a tease!"

Grapes giggle, dressed in purple hue,
"This royal fruit can't handle dew!
He slips and slides with such delight,
Oh, can't we keep this from his sight?"

So if you roam where fruits convene,
Listen close, but do not preen.
For secrets swirl with every breeze,
In the orchard, we're all just peas!

Winds of Change in the Grove

The winds are wild, the branches sway,
"Hey there, fruit! What do you say?"
A pear replied with a quirky grin,
"Let's spin around, let's begin!"

The apples laughed, they tumbled down,
"I'll bounce right up, from this here crown!"
With every gust, the fruits took flight,
"Come join our dance!" they shouted in might.

A fig chimed in, "Don't be a bore,
Whee! Let's twirl just a little more!"
The oranges jived with zest and glow,
"Let's shake it off, let our spirits flow!"

So when the breezes start to sing,
And trees jiggle in a joyful fling,
Remember, friends, the fruits are bold,
With winds of change, their tales unfold!

Routes to Forked Futures

In the orchard, fruits collide,
Plans made under trees so wide.
One goes left, the other right,
Choosing paths in morning light.

A hasty pear made quite the scene,
Said, "I'll wear a crown, you'll wear green!"
But tripping on an apple core,
Said, "I'll stick to the fashion store!"

Lemons laughed from leafy heights,
"Who knew fruits had such delights?"
They spread rumors, fresh and sweet,
About oranges with two left feet!

So thus they sprout with plans so grand,
Dreaming of a fruit-filled land.
Paths entwined in laughter true,
Who knew a pear could wear a shoe?

Nature's Endearing Commitments

Amidst the blooms and buzzing bees,
A vow was made with silly ease.
"I'll grow a mustache, you a hat!"
The cherries giggled, "Oh, imagine that!"

A cabbage rolled with leafy dreams,
While peas plotted in clever schemes.
"We'll host a ball, you bring a dance!"
The veggies laughed, not missing chance!

Tomatoes blushed in sunlit glades,
Said, "We'll serenade, but no charades!"
With every slice and every beat,
Their funny antics can't be beat!

So from the soil, the laughter grows,
In nature's world, hilarity flows.
Through every sprout and every cheer,
They keep their bonds, forever near.

The Glow of Anticipated Fruit

With every sunrise, the garden glows,
Anxious fruits, they come and pose.
"I'm ripe for joy!" a peach exclaimed,
"But wait! Is it time?" a fig complained.

A banana slipped on morning dew,
While kiwi played peekaboo.
"I'm not shy, I'll wait my turn!"
Said every fruit with zest to learn!

A pomegranate burst with glee,
Said, "Patience is the key for me!"
While cherries counted down the days,
To show off their red, adorable ways!

So as the harvest draws near,
The garden bursts with throaty cheer.
Each fruit embraces the coming fate,
With laughter ringing, never late.

Journeys Sprouting from the Earth

From the soil, a sprout takes flight,
Wondering what lies out of sight.
With roots that tickle, it stretches high,
"Will I be dinner or just a pie?"

Mushrooms danced in moonlit haze,
While carrots plotted sneaky ways.
"Let's escape to the farmer's truck!"
They dreamed of rides, oh what a luck!

But sprouts were wise, made a firm stand,
"Don't rush us, we've got dreams so grand!"
The radishes giggled, "You'll be amazed,
When you see how the world is glazed!"

So sprouting tales of what could be,
They set their sights on the big blue sea.
With every inch, they laughed with glee,
"The world's our stage, just wait and see!"

When Saplings Sing Softly

In a garden where whispers play,
Little sprouts giggle all day.
They dance in the breeze with flair,
Waving their leaves without a care.

The sun peeks in with a cheeky grin,
As worms wiggle and join in.
Each little leaf has a secret to share,
Of dreams and adventures beyond compare.

With each drop of rain, they jump with glee,
Planning a party under the tree.
The soil's their stage, the roots their crew,
Oh, what a sight when the soft winds blew!

So laugh with the sprouts, let your heart sing,
For life is a joke that nature will bring.
In the garden of giggles, let's all partake,
Join the saplings in their merry make-believe break.

Echoes of Abundant Springs

Once in a glade, the apples conspired,
To spill all their secrets, they were inspired.
With nuts that would gossip, and berries so bold,
They'd scheme for a feast as the stories unfold.

The cherries chuckled, their colors so bright,
Plotting a party each warm summer night.
"We'll invite all the fruits, and even the bees,
With music from crickets, and light from the leaves!"

But the pears just sighed, sat back, and pretended,
"Maturity's boring," they casually blended.
Yet deep down inside, with a twinkle in sight,
They'd giggle and wait for their time in the light.

So listen close, through the laughter and springs,
For echoes of joy hide in natural things.
In a world filled with pranks, mischief will bloom,
Even ripe little ones shake off their gloom.

A Harvest Yet to Come

A little green fruit hung high on a bough,
Dreaming of days when she'd take her first bow.
"I'll be the star at the big harvest feast,
But first I must hang here, at least!"

With a wink from the sun and a breeze in a whirl,
She pondered each moment, her bright future unfurled.
"What if I'm picked and there's pie? Oh dear!
I'd rather be juice, it's a far better sphere!"

Yet each day she grew, in the sun's warm embrace,
Wondering who'd love her sweet, tender taste.
Candied or canned, with a delicate edge,
Oh, the thrill of that moment, a tasty hedge!

So here's to the waiting, the laugh and the tease,
Of fruits and their plans, caught in playful breeze.
For a harvest to come is a joke yet to tell,
Full of surprises, and a sweetness swell!

Dreaming in Soft Hues

In twilight's embrace, under stars so bright,
Fruits whisper their dreams in the cool of the night.
"Someday I'll shimmer in colors galore,
From lime to the lilac, oh, what's to explore?"

Each berry and peach joined in with a cheer,
Imagining flavors that would bring joy near.
With flavors exploding, like fireworks' show,
They giggled and twinkled while watching the glow.

A banana in yellow, with a mischievous grin,
Scribbled sweet tales of the fun that begins.
And the grapes laughed with glee, knowing they'd find,
Their journeys to wine and good times intertwined.

So, here's to the dreams that we all carry slow,
In shades that we wear, in hues that we know.
The world holds us dear in its whimsical tide,
As we laugh with our colors, and take life in stride.

Beneath the Boughs

Under the tree, we giggle and sway,
Leaves rustle softly, in the most silly way.
A droopy fruit waves, it's slipping our sight,
Whispers of sweetness, oh what a delight!

With every step, we dodge with a laugh,
The cheeky little branches, they play a rough craft.
A pear drops down, we think it's a game,
Who knew gardening would end with such fame?

We point and we tease at the ripe harvest there,
Yet trip on roots, oh, watch out for your hair!
Laughing so hard, it's nature's grand jest,
In the orchard of giggles, we're truly blessed!

So here beneath boughs, we find our delight,
In fruits that remind us, not all is polite.
With every mishap, we cherish the fun,
As the garden keeps laughing, and so do we run!

Hope Grows

In the patchy rows, our thoughts take to flight,
We dream of the future, oh, what a sight!
A whisper from roots, it tickles our feet,
Yells of tomorrow with every heartbeat!

A tiny seedling peeks, with a grin so wide,
Trying to look bold with nothing to hide.
We cheer it on loudly, "You're doing just fine!"
Bouncing in soil, that's our little sign!

Sprouts shaking their heads, like they're caught in a trance,
We revel in growth, as if caught in a dance.
Little quirks abound, it's a whimsical show,
Nature's own circus, where hope truly grows!

So here we stand, with laughter and cheer,
Each day in this garden, our dreams reappear.
With roots intertwined, our joy will not cease,
For in every green shoot, there's a little piece of peace!

Tender Moments in the Garden

Among the flowers, we whisper and play,
Telling the petals to brighten the day.
With each bloom's chuckle, we join in the jest,
Here in our garden, we feel truly blessed!

One flower is shy, with its head kind of low,
We tickle its stem, "Come on, let's go!"
In this patch of giggles, the moments are sweet,
Every laugh shared, makes our joy feel complete.

The veggies join in with a cabbage parade,
Zucchini winks slyly, unafraid to invade.
"Lettuce all dance!" is the chant that we hear,
As we twirl with laughter, the sun's shining clear!

So tender the moments, we gather them near,
These silly little snippets, so priceless, so dear.
With petals and laughter, our hearts feel the spark,
In the garden of giggles, we leave our sweet mark!

Shadows of an Unseen Bloom

In the twilight hour, we wander around,
Where shadows of flowers begin to abound.
Each petal that shifts, tells a tale that's untold,
Of secrets and laughter that slowly unfold!

We spot a small bunny, with ears oh so tall,
Hiding from flowers, it's a game, that's the call!
We giggle and whisper, "Where did you go?"
As shadows dance lightly, in the evening's soft glow.

A green vine climbs high, with dreams made of cheer,
Swaying in rhythm, it joins the fun near.
Mirth grows in silence, as we scheme and we plot,
Crafting the joy in this magical spot!

So here in the dusk, where glee intertwines,
We sip from the laughter, with no need for signs.
In shadows of blooms, we know we are free,
In moments of mischief, just you wait, and you'll see!

Nature's Gentle Vow

With a twinkle of dew, the morning awakes,
Nature's soft laughter, for goodness' sakes!
A squirrel darts by with a nut in its cheek,
Pledging allegiance to this whimsical peak.

The flowers are waving, they flourish and sway,
Making promises for a bountiful day.
And in every bud, there's a humorous spark,
Each one a giggler, igniting the park!

"Let's play a game of hide and seek!"
The ferns whisper softly, as they start to squeak.
Moments of joy, in the crisp morning air,
Nature's own laughter, we cherish and share.

So here with the blooms and the buzzing of bees,
We dance through the meadow, at ease in the breeze.
Nature has promised a world filled with fun,
In giggles and grins, we're never outdone!

www.ingramcontent.com/pod-product-compliance
Lightning Source LLC
Chambersburg PA
CBHW060147230426
43661CB00003B/598